STENCIL IT!

SALLY & STEWART WALTON

Sterling Publishing Co., Inc.   New York

Library of Congress Cataloging-in-Publication Data

Walton, Sally.
    Stencil It: over 100 step-by-step projects / Sally & Stewart Walton
        p.   cm.
    Summary: Presents techniques for stencilling stationery, borders, hats,
masks, cake decorations, and other projects. Includes templates.
    ISBN 0-8069-0346-5
    1. Stencil work – Juvenile literature. [1. Stencil work. 2. Handicraft.]
1. Walton, Stewart.   II. Title.
TT270.W35   1992
745.7′3 – dc20   92-36177
                                                      CIP
                                                       AC

Designer: Janet James
Editor: Penny Horton

1 3 5 7 9 10 8 6 4 2

Published 1993 by Sterling Publishing Company, Inc.
387 Park Avenue South, New York, N.Y. 10016
Originally published in Great Britain by
Simon & Schuster Young Books Ltd
Created for Simon & Schuster Young Books
and © 1992 by Amazon Publishing Ltd
Text and artwork © 1992 by Sally and Stewart Walton
Distributed in Canada by Sterling Publishing
c/o Canadian Manda Group, P.O. Box 920, Station U
Toronto, Ontario, Canada M8Z SP9
Printed and Bound in Hong Kong
All rights reserved

Sterling ISBN 0-8069-0346-5

Contents

Stencil Starter

Stenciling is very easy and is great fun. If you have never used a stencil before, then prepare yourself for a treat. But allow yourself plenty of time, because once you start, you just can't stop.

Stenciling is a simple way of repeating shapes and making patterns that has been popular for thousands of years. A stencil is really just a piece of poster board with a shape cut out of it. The poster board is placed on the surface that you want to decorate so that you can paint in the shape.

Women in the South Seas even used banana leaves to make stencils and painted through them onto cloth. But we suggest that you use thin poster board for yours!

Never be afraid to try out a stencil. You don't have to make a perfect job of it. A row of stenciled flowers will look good even if some are a bit smudged around the edges. Remember that a machine would print 40 daisies exactly the same, but everyone will know it is handmade if each one is slightly different.

Stencil Kit

You can begin stenciling right away, without spending lots of money on equipment. You will probably have most of the materials on this list, but you may need to buy a few. All of them can be bought from an arts and crafts store.

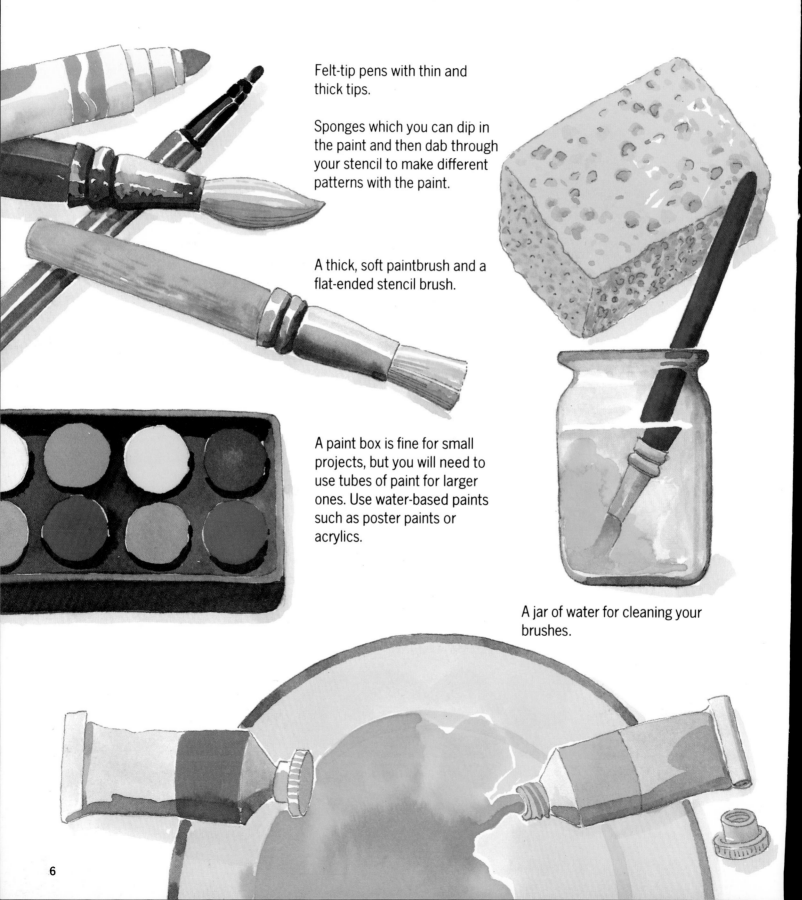

Felt-tip pens with thin and thick tips.

Sponges which you can dip in the paint and then dab through your stencil to make different patterns with the paint.

A thick, soft paintbrush and a flat-ended stencil brush.

A paint box is fine for small projects, but you will need to use tubes of paint for larger ones. Use water-based paints such as poster paints or acrylics.

A jar of water for cleaning your brushes.

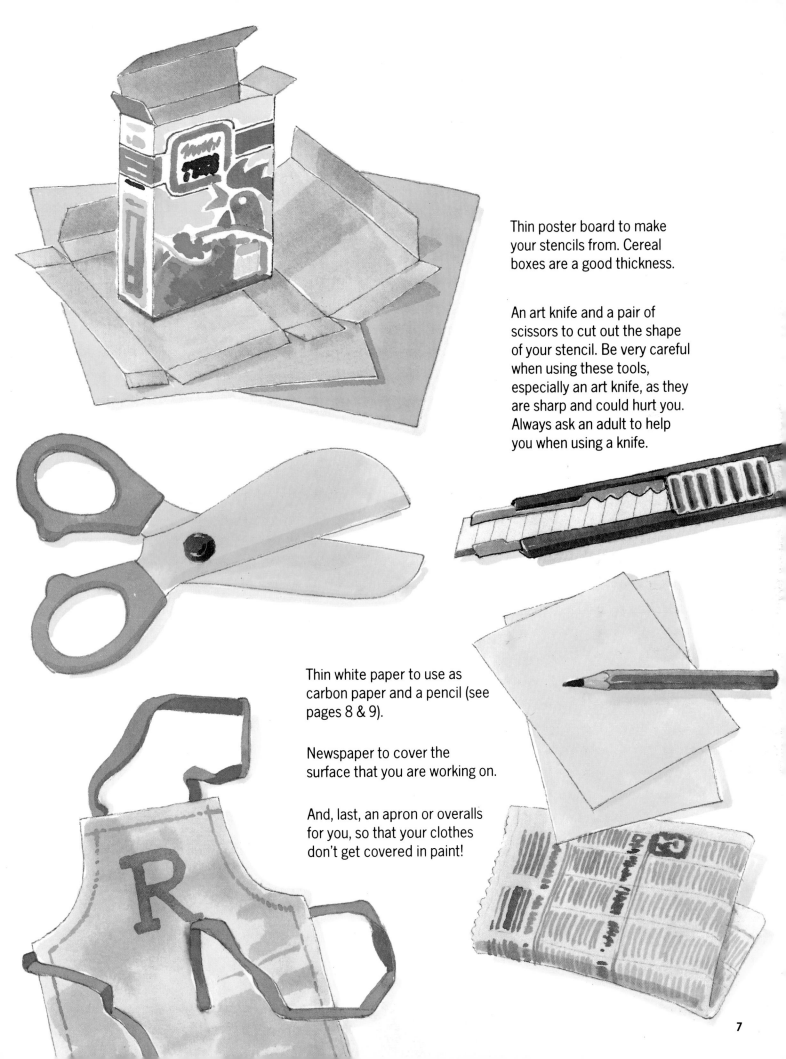

Thin poster board to make your stencils from. Cereal boxes are a good thickness.

An art knife and a pair of scissors to cut out the shape of your stencil. Be very careful when using these tools, especially an art knife, as they are sharp and could hurt you. Always ask an adult to help you when using a knife.

Thin white paper to use as carbon paper and a pencil (see pages 8 & 9).

Newspaper to cover the surface that you are working on.

And, last, an apron or overalls for you, so that your clothes don't get covered in paint!

Copying Stencils

Look through the book and choose a stencil that you like. Start with a shape that will be easy to cut out. You will find the stencil shapes at the back of the book — this symbol STENCILS p 68 tells you which pages to look at. You may want to ask an adult to make the stencil shape bigger or smaller on a photocopier.

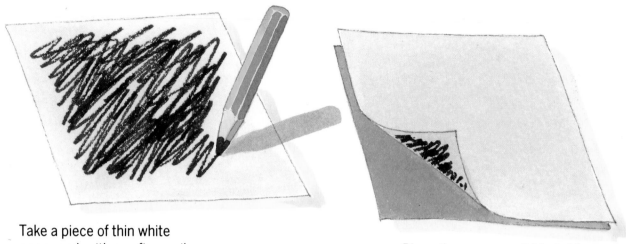

Take a piece of thin white paper and, with a soft pencil, scribble all over one side of it.

Place the paper, scribbled-side down, on a piece of thin poster board the same size.

Tuck the paper and poster board into the book on the page after the one with your stencil on it.

Smooth the page over the paper and poster board.

Now draw around the stencil in the book with a pencil or a ballpoint pen. You will need to press quite hard to make sure that the stencil comes through on the poster board.

If you have borrowed this book from a library and do not want to draw on the pages, just put a piece of tracing paper over the stencil shape before you draw around it. The result will be exactly the same.

Before you remove the poster board, peep under one edge of the paper to check that the stencil is now on the card. If not, just go over it again.

Cutting a Stencil

Trim down your stencil with scissors, leaving at least a 2″ (five centimeter) border all the way around your pattern.

The finished dove stencil.

Cut the stencil from the middle out toward the edges. When you reach an edge, don't try to turn the scissors. Go back to the middle and cut outward again.

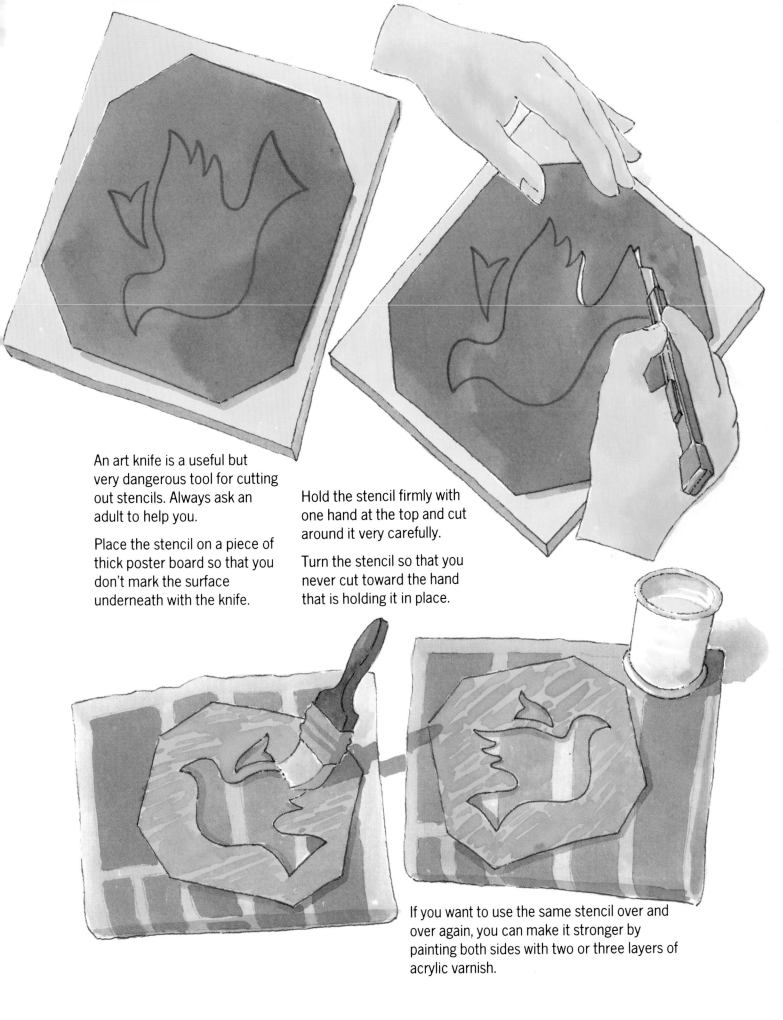

An art knife is a useful but very dangerous tool for cutting out stencils. Always ask an adult to help you.

Place the stencil on a piece of thick poster board so that you don't mark the surface underneath with the knife.

Hold the stencil firmly with one hand at the top and cut around it very carefully.

Turn the stencil so that you never cut toward the hand that is holding it in place.

If you want to use the same stencil over and over again, you can make it stronger by painting both sides with two or three layers of acrylic varnish.

Start Stenciling!

A little paint goes a long way. Try painting onto scrap paper first to make sure that you haven't got too much paint on your brush.

Hold your stencil still with your spare hand, or use a bit of masking tape to keep the stencil in place.

Make sure that the paint is quite thick. Watery paint will leak under your stencil.

Paint around the inside edges and then the middle.

The paint can be less thick when you use a sponge, because it will soak a lot up.

Use a light dabbing movement when you paint.

For no-mess stenciling, use a felt-tip pen.

Make sure you fill in around the edges as well as in the middle.

Remove the stencil very carefully so that you don't smudge the paint or felt-tip pen. Wipe off the wet paint from the edges of the stencil with a tissue or slightly damp cloth. You will then have a clean stencil to use again.

When you use a paintbrush, let the brush marks show – it's all part of the special stencil look!

Using a sponge gives a spotty texture. It does not need to be even all over.

The quickest way to stencil is with a felt-tip pen – you can make a great picture in seconds!

Mail a Picture

You can make your own stationery by stenciling paper, envelopes and notecards with a favorite design. Decorated envelopes are fun to make and fun to receive. They also cheer up the person who delivers the mail!

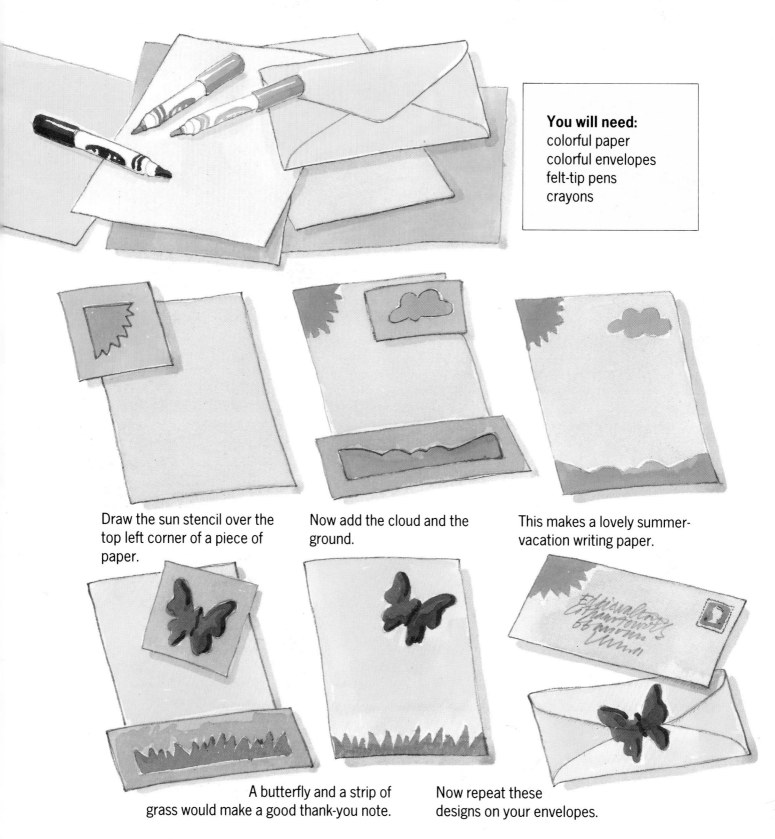

You will need:
colorful paper
colorful envelopes
felt-tip pens
crayons

Draw the sun stencil over the top left corner of a piece of paper.

Now add the cloud and the ground.

This makes a lovely summer-vacation writing paper.

A butterfly and a strip of grass would make a good thank-you note.

Now repeat these designs on your envelopes.

STENCILS pp 65–66

Here are two border designs to choose from. You can stencil the top and bottom edges and the sides as well. Just remember to leave plenty of room to write your letters.

Notecards can be made from one piece of paper.

Fold the paper in half, from top to bottom.

Fold in half again, from left to right.

Stencil your design on the front, so that you have lots of room inside to write your letter.

Colorful Cards

Treat your friends to a homemade card instead of an expensive one from a store. There are lots of ideas here for cards to send on birthdays, at Christmas and for other special occasions.

You will need:	paintbrush	felt-tip pens	envelopes	glue
	poster board	paints	ruler	glitter

Envelopes come in different shapes and sizes, so, start with the envelope and make your card to fit.

This pattern of simple shapes has been painted in two colors.

First, stencil the heart in red and then use the smaller stencil over it in purple.

These five simple shapes can be used in many different ways. Change the background colors using different-color paper or paints. Try stenciling with glue and adding glitter (see page 18).

This dove card would suit most occasions.

Stencils are great for making a matching set of cards.
But using different background colors makes them more interesting.

Three Christmas card ideas

Start by stenciling a border in two colors.

STENCILS pp 65 · 67 · 68 · 69

When the paint is dry, stencil the center with either the tree or the holly. Have a brush for each color to avoid mixing the green and the red.

Stencil the star with glue, take off the stencil and sprinkle with glitter.

Lift it carefully and tap the back over a sheet of paper to shake off the loose glitter.

Fold a piece of poster board 16″ long and 5″ high (40 centimeters long and 12 centimeters high), in half from left to right.

Take each end and fold it back to the crease of the first fold.

Stencil an engine at one end with three cars behind it.

You could draw faces at the windows.

The butterfly stencil can be used alone, in pairs, or with the flower.

19

All Wrapped Up

**Presents look lovely wrapped in special paper, but it is expensive to buy.
You can make lots of unusual wrapping paper with stencils.
Here are nine designs for you to copy and some ideas for gift tags too!**

You will need:

colored paper	paintbrushes
brown wrapping	felt-tip pens
paper	sponge
tissue paper	newspaper
crepe paper	string or ribbon
paints	hole puncher
	scissors

Cover a large working surface with newspaper to avoid mess.

Use quite thin paper, as thick paper won't fold well around packages.

Red roses show up well on green paper.

Paint bows in pretty pastel colors.

STENCILS p 68

Light gray water splashes look great on a darker background.

Red stars look good in rows.

Scatter kisses all over pink paper.

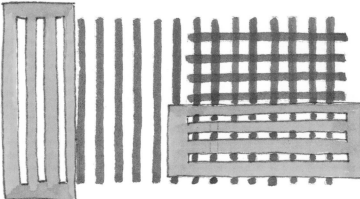

Paint stripes downward on a sheet of pink paper.

When dry, turn the stencil and paint across them to make checks.

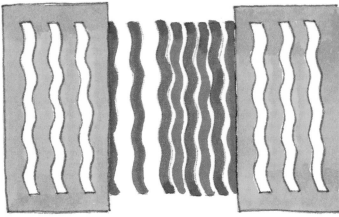

The background color is light green.

Paint the red wiggly lines through the stencil.

When the paint is dry, move the stencil across so that you can paint the green lines.

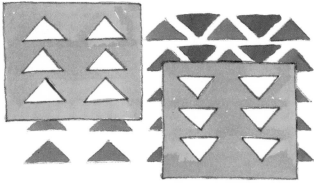

This stencil is used pointed-end up for the green triangles and turned pointed-end down to paint the red ones.

STENCILS p 70

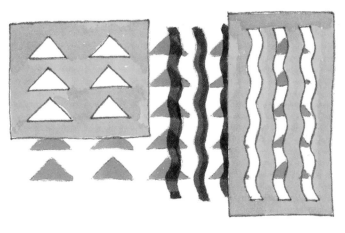

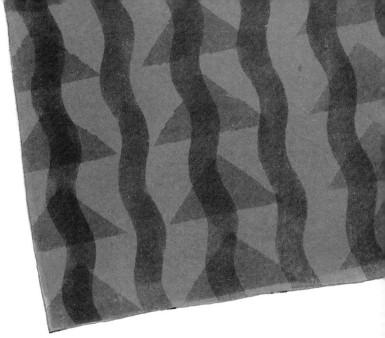

On purple paper, stencil rows of triangles. Then paint stripes of wiggly lines between and through the pattern in a dark purple.

Gift tags can be made from scraps of poster board. Square ones look good but you can vary the shapes by snipping off corners or cutting around your stenciled design.

Make a neat hole with a hole puncher and thread a piece of string or ribbon through the hole.

Party Time!

Paper tablecloths and napkins can be bought in different colors which you can decorate with your own stencil designs to make your parties really special.

You will need:
paper tablecloths
paper napkins
acrylic paints
paintbrush
glue
glitter

Make a stencil of a birthday cake and a birthday candle.

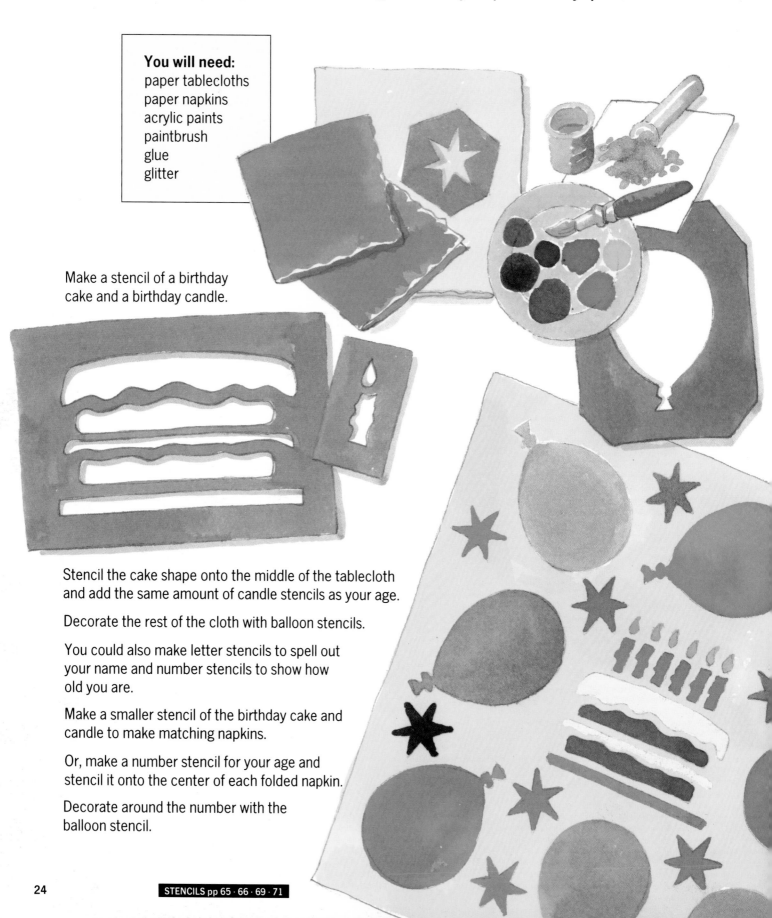

Stencil the cake shape onto the middle of the tablecloth and add the same amount of candle stencils as your age.

Decorate the rest of the cloth with balloon stencils.

You could also make letter stencils to spell out your name and number stencils to show how old you are.

Make a smaller stencil of the birthday cake and candle to make matching napkins.

Or, make a number stencil for your age and stencil it onto the center of each folded napkin.

Decorate around the number with the balloon stencil.

STENCILS pp 65 · 66 · 69 · 71

Make a large
Christmas-tree stencil.

Place it in the center of a red
or green paper tablecloth.

Fill in the shape with a layer of
paper glue and while the glue
is still wet, sprinkle with gold or
silver glitter.

When the glue is dry, shake the
cloth over some newspaper to
get rid of any extra glitter.

Decorate the rest of the cloth
with the bell stencil.

Use the bell stencil to make
matching napkins.

25

Party Goodies

You don't need to be an expert baker to change plain cakes and cookies into party food.

You will need:
a plain chocolate cake
jam or whipped cream
plain cookies
food coloring
confectioners' sugar
chocolate powder
cake-decorating gel
a sieve

Place the stencil on top of the cake.

Put a spoonful of confectioners' sugar into the sieve and gently shake it over the stencil.

When no more cake shows through the stencil, remove the stencil very carefully.

Fill the middle of the cake with jam or whipped cream before you decorate it.

To cover the cake top with hearts, hold the stencil just above the cake when you sieve the confectioners' sugar over it.

Move the stencil carefully and repeat until there are no more spaces.

Don't touch the cake with the stencil as this will smudge your pattern.

STENCILS p 72

Coat the cookies with icing.

To decorate plain cookies you will need to make icing. Ask an adult to help you.

Mix one tablespoon of hot water with four tablespoons of confectioners' sugar. Stir until smooth. Add a drop of coloring and stir again.

Hold your stencil just above a cookie and sieve on confectioners' sugar or chocolate powder.

Remove the stencil and outline the shape with colored cake-decorating gel.

Fly the Flag

Each nation has its own flag and not one is the same as another. There are also company, club and team flags. Ships use a code made up of flags of different shapes, sizes and colors, to signal to each other. You can make flags to decorate your classroom or school yard for Sports Day, or for a party at home.

You will need:

thin poster board	paper glue
paints	thin sticks
felt-tip pens	pencil and ruler
paintbrushes	string or wool
masking tape	scissors

Cut the card into a rectangle, about 6" by 4" (15 centimeters by 10 centimeters).

Stencil the cross at one end.

When it is dry, turn it over and paint the other side to match.

Tape the stick to the flag and fold the end of the poster board over. Tape it down for a neat finish.

STENCILS pp 67 · 72

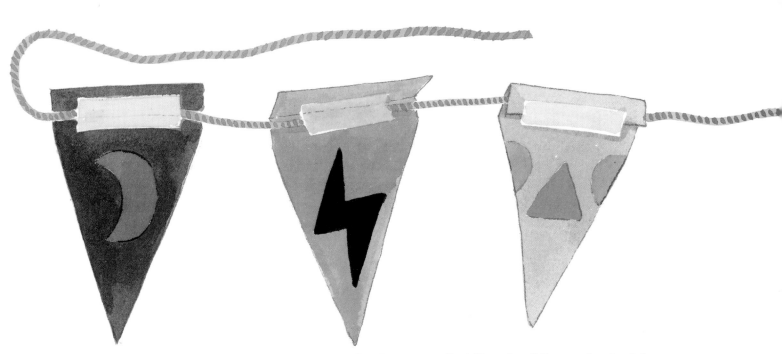

Rows of triangular flags on a piece of string are called "bunting." Rows of colorful bunting would brighten up any event.

Choose a few simple shapes to decorate your flags and go wild with as many colors as you like.

Copy the pattern of our triangular shape. Cut out lots of flags the same size.

When the paint is dry, tape the flags to a length of string or wool. Fold the ends over and tape them down.

Try copying your own national flag or make one up for your family or group of friends.

Painting Pictures

Be a great painter using stencils to make colorful paintings for your walls.
Stenciled paintings were very popular in America a long time ago. They were
known as "Theorem" paintings.
Don't forget you can turn the stencils over and use them facing the other way.

You will need:
paints
paper
paintbrushes
felt-tip pens
sponge

There are flower, stalk, leaf
and grass stencils for you to
arrange in different ways. You
can mix brush strokes with
sponged paint and felt-tip pens
in the same picture. Use lots
of bright colors to make a
painting that will cheer up any
wall.

STENCILS p 73

A paddle steamer, a tribal pattern or a very silly bird are just a few ideas for paintings that you can make from stencils. Experiment with colors, shapes and textures.

Make all the stencils on this page and move them around on a piece of paper. See what patterns and pictures you can make up.

STENCILS p 73

Mounting Paintings

Most artists have their paintings framed to make sure that they look their best. These picture mounts are cardboard frames which are great for photographs, paintings or your favorite pictures.

You will need:
thick mounting
    cardboard
short pieces of string
masking tape
glue stick
felt-tip pens
paints
painbrushes

Put your picture down on top of the cardboard.

Move it around until all the border edges look the same.

Draw around the corners of your picture with a pencil to mark its place on the card.

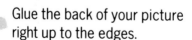

Glue the back of your picture right up to the edges.

Carefully stick your picture to the mount using your pencil marks to position it correctly.

Diamonds, double wavy lines and the chunky comb shape all make good border patterns.

Take your picture away and stencil the border.

STENCILS pp 70 · 73 · 74

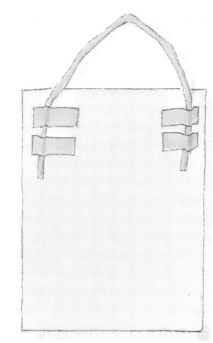

Turn the picture and mount over.

Take a short piece of string and position each end about 2″ (five centimeters) from either edge, near the top of the mount.

Stick the string in place with masking tape.

Ask an adult to pound a nail into the wall of your choice so that you can hang your picture.

Identikits

Have you ever wondered how it is that with two eyes, two ears, eyebrows, a nose and a mouth, we all manage to look so different? Hairstyles, mustaches, hats and bow ties add even more variety. Have fun with these identikits and see just how many different characters you can make. You could be a cowboy, clown, teacher, rock star or even a bank robber!

You will need:

paper plates	felt-tip pens
paints	ribbon or string
paintbrushes	skewer

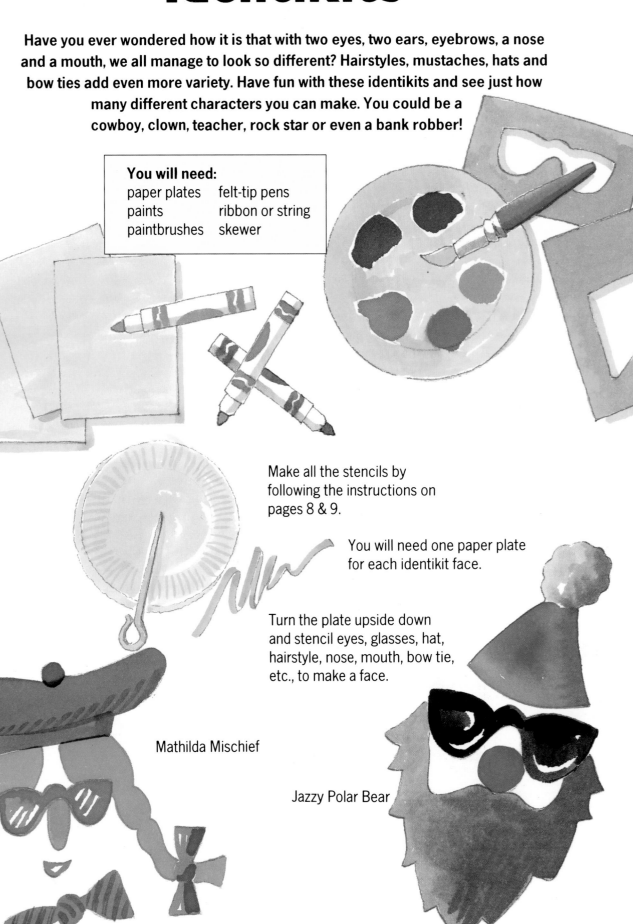

Make all the stencils by following the instructions on pages 8 & 9.

You will need one paper plate for each identikit face.

Turn the plate upside down and stencil eyes, glasses, hat, hairstyle, nose, mouth, bow tie, etc., to make a face.

Mathilda Mischief

Jazzy Polar Bear

36

STENCILS pp 74 · 75

Bank Robber

Clown

Cowboy

Three characters all wearing the same hat.

When you have finished your face and the paint is dry, ask an adult to help you to pierce two holes with a skewer at the top of the plate. Thread a piece of ribbon through each one. Tie the ribbon together to make a loop. Now you can hang your plate picture on the wall.

Mr. McHaggis

Miss Polly Pink

Fancy Dress Hats and Masks

Be a king or queen, a pirate or a member of a carnival procession, with a handmade hat or mask.

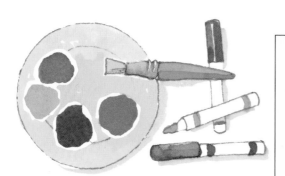

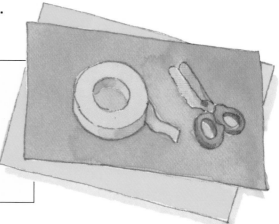

You will need:

tape measure	pencil
thin poster	ruler
board	masking tape
paints	scissors
paintbrushes	a stapler
felt-tip pens	ribbon

Measure your head with a tape measure, at the point where a hat would sit comfortably.

Cut out a piece of gold or silver poster board the same length, and about 5″ (12 centimeters) in height.

Stencil the crown shape along the length of the poster board, one next to the other.

Cut the shape around the top of the crown with a pair of scissors.

Try the crown for size and then stick the two ends of the strip together with masking tape.

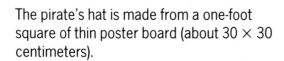

The pirate's hat is made from a one-foot square of thin poster board (about 30 × 30 centimeters).

With a pencil and ruler draw a straight line from one corner, across the square, to the opposite corner.

Cut along this line with scissors.

Place the two triangles together and staple along the two shorter edges.

Try the hat on and pinch the brim edges together with your fingers so that it fits your head.

Mark these two points with a pencil and staple the brim edges together up to these marks on either side.

Stencil the skull and crossbones onto both sides of your hat.

Masks

Draw the shape of the mask onto a piece of poster board and decorate it with stripes before you cut it out.

Ask an adult to make the eye holes for you.

Use staples to fix the ribbons to the sides of your mask.

These two shapes can be decorated in all sorts of ways. Try using some glue and glitter for a sparkly mask.

Three very bright and different masks

The Family Tree

A family tree is something to keep and treasure. It records your name and birth date and the names of your parents, grandparents and great-grandparents with their birth dates.

A blank tree makes a good present for a friend or new parents to fill in.

You will need:
pencil
paints
paintbrush
a sheet of good paper
your best pen

Start at the bottom of the page and stencil your tree in pencil.

Paint the tree and the birds.

Paint the leafy areas in a light green so that your writing will show up on top of it.

Make sure the paint is bone dry before you add the names and dates.

Write each name and date out first on scrap paper. This way you will see how much space it takes up and be able to place it neatly in the center of each leafy area.

When you are ready, write the names and dates in the correct spaces with your best pen.

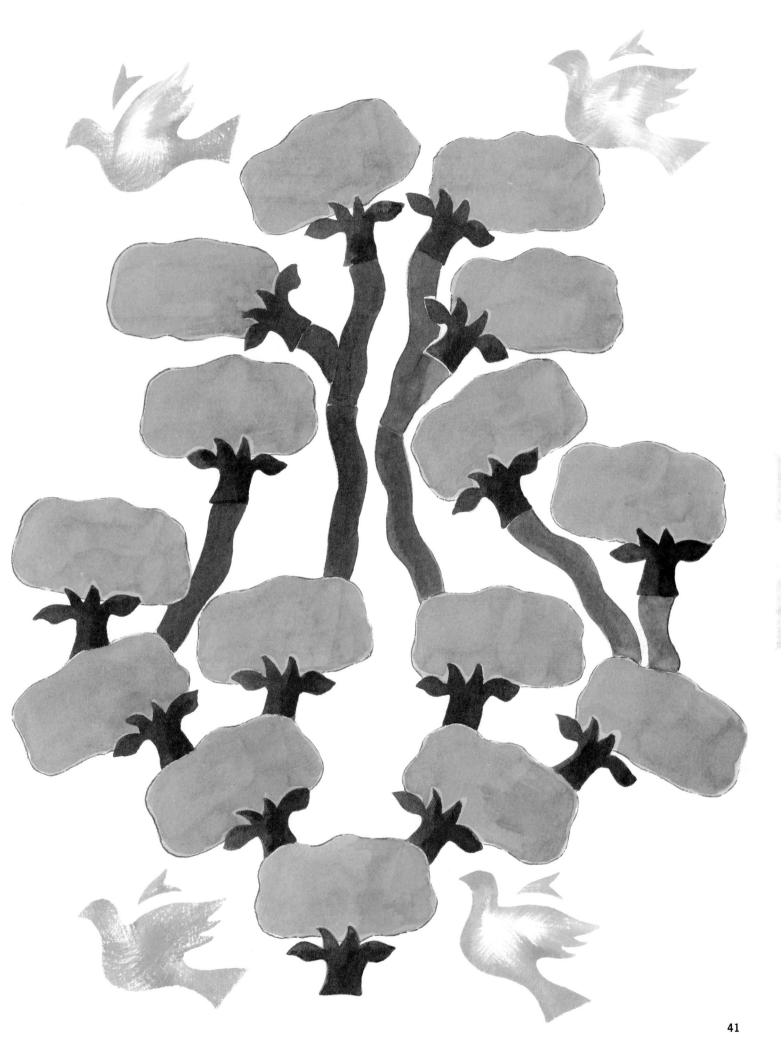

41

Farmyard Fun

Cock-a-doodle-do! Old MacDonald would feel quite at home in this stenciled farmyard! Would you like to have your own farmyard? Using as many of the ideas as you like, and a few of your own, you can make a simpler farm or a much bigger one.

STENCILS pp 76·77·78

43

Choose a strong cardboard box to make the farmhouse.

Ask an adult to cut it into shape using the drawing as a guide.

Paint the box all one color and stencil the windows and the roof tiles.

To make the porch, cut a long thin piece of poster board and divide it in six, as shown in the plan.

Take a ruler and a knitting needle and draw a line with the needle wherever there is a red dotted line in our drawings.

This will make it easier to fold the poster board. This is called scoring.

The measurements will depend on the size of your house, so use ours as a guide.

Overlap the end sections and glue them together. Cut a square of poster board as a base and stick the porch onto it.

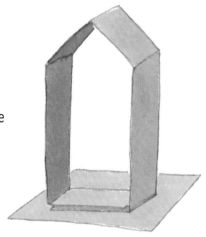

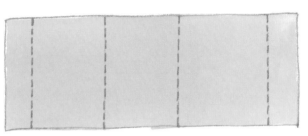

The storeroom is made by scoring and folding a rectangular piece of poster board as shown in the drawing.

Paint it the same color as the farmhouse and use glue to stick it to one of the side walls.

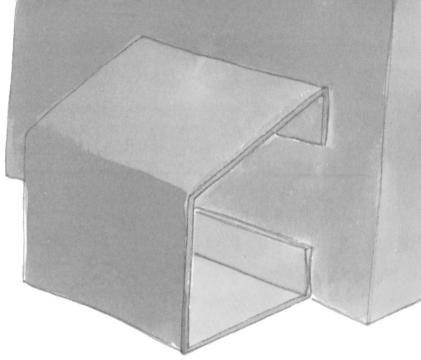

The pigsty is cut from a single piece of card.

Ask an adult to draw it out from the plan, enlarging it to suit the size of your farm.

Score along the dotted lines and fold them.

The two end sections are glued together to make a double-thickness front wall.

The roof is folded down to meet the sides.

Paint the sty in a plain color and use the stone stencil to decorate.

The barn is also made from a cardboard box and has a door cut in one end.

Ask an adult to cut it out for you and then paint it white.

Use the stone stencil to paint the barn walls, and paint the door black.

Paint the roof bright yellow first. Add orange stripes for the straw thatch.

The stencils will give you the shape of the animals and you can follow our examples when you paint them. It is very easy to make the animals stand up using a slotted stand. Try it once and you will soon have a whole herd.

Cut out a stand for the sheep.

Cut it out and paint the other side. Draw the legs, tail, face and ears in felt-tip pen.

Stencil a sheep onto thin poster board.

Now you can make all the other animals.

Now cut the slots, both the same length, and slide them together.

Paint the horse a chestnut color, dappled gray or black.

The billy-goat can have a patch of grass to nibble.

Make lots of hens so that you can put them all around the farmyard.

This fat pink pig has its own sty. Don't forget to add the curly tail.

You can really enjoy painting this bright rooster.

Paint a blue pond for the ducks to swim on.

Your cows could be brown or black and white. Choose your favorite type of cow and paint them all the same.

The tree has a special trunk-shaped stand which is painted to match. Try stenciling red apples on a tree.

47

DIY Dollhouse

This lovely dollhouse is made from two cardboard boxes and will be strong enough to last for years. It will take time to make and would be a good holiday project.

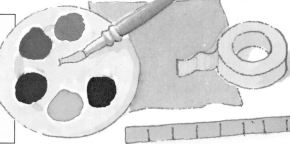

You will need:
two identical boxes, very strong paper glue, extra cardboard for the roof and the base, masking tape, paints, paintbrushes, felt-tip pens, sponge

Ask an adult to make the house with you. Study the drawing, which shows just how the house is put together.

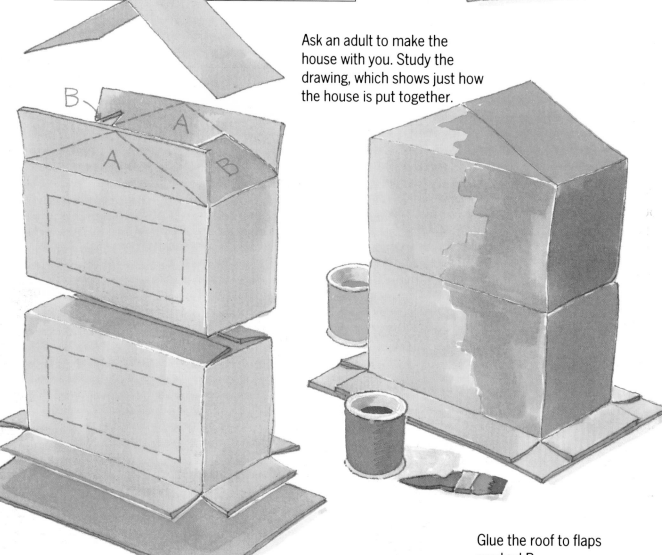

Glue the two closed ends of the boxes together.

Cut the corners off flaps marked A.

Cut a roof the same width as flap B and long enough to cover the house. Fold it in the middle and rest it on the top of the house.

Glue the roof to flaps marked B.

Glue the house to the base using the folded-out flaps.

Cut out the back of the house, as shown by the dotted line.

Paint the house and the roof.

STENCILS pp 70 · 76 · 78

The roof tiles are stenciled with a red felt-tip pen. Begin at the top of the roof and work downward.

Paint a light-colored background for the windows and door. Use the guide on p. 78 to make a rectangle to draw around for the windows, then just make it longer for the door.

Practice on scrap paper before you start stenciling the brickwork. It is easy once you get the idea.

Look at the top of the house — it shows the finished brickwork. The bottom section has only half of the bricks.

The stencil is being used to draw the rows in between.

These rows of bricks are drawn under the spaces in between the row above. This gives the brickwork effect.

Stencil the porch and window-panes in a dark color.

This is what the dollhouse will look like when you start adding the windowpanes.

Let the windows dry and then add the porch.

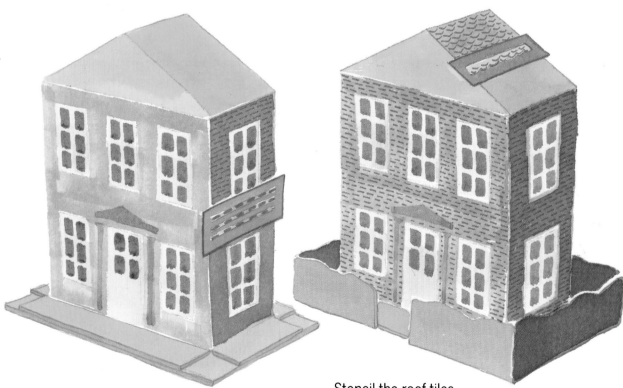

Begin stenciling the brickwork on one of the sides.

Take care not to stencil over the window frames.

Stencil the roof tiles.

Measure the base and cut a hedge shape to go around it.

Paint it green with a sponge.

One last thing – paint a number on the door.

Make Your Own Map

You can follow this plan to make your own map, or make one up. You could even make a map of where you live.

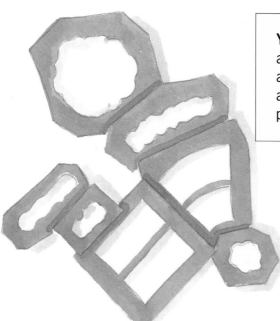

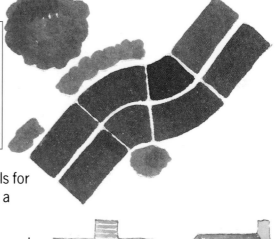

> **You will need:**
> a large sheet of fiberboard
> acrylic paints
> acrylic varnish
> paintbrushes

There are just two stencils for the road – a straight and a curve.

To make this bend in the road the curved stencil is used on both sides, next to each other.

Six of the curves will make a traffic circle.

There are three stages in painting a map.

Begin by roughly marking out your roads in pencil.

The next stage is to paint the roads, parking lots and traffic circles in gray, with a white center line.

Now paint the background pale green and then add hedges and trees in a darker green.

Make as many of the stencils as you like.

We have decorated our map with houses (use the drawings above as a guide) and a pond, but you can add lots of different things such as a river, a farm, shops, cars and buses, a railroad station or a school.

Place trees, farm animals, etc., all over the map, using stencils from the rest of the book.

Now, think of a name for your made-up place.

STENCILS p 79

Amazing Mats!

Brighten up your family dinner table with a set of stenciled table mats and coasters.

> **You will need:**
> cork floor tiles   acrylic paint   paintbrushes
> felt for backing   white glue   acrylic varnish

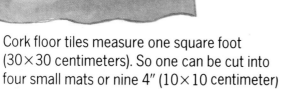

Cork floor tiles measure one square foot (30×30 centimeters). So one can be cut into four small mats or nine 4″ (10×10 centimeter) coasters.

Ask an adult to cut two tiles in four for you, so that you can make eight table mats.

Stencil the rose in the middle of each mat.

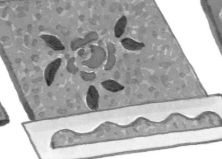

Use the wavy line stencil right on the edges.

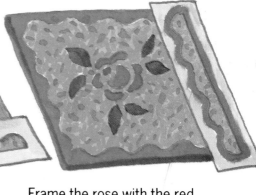

Frame the rose with the red wavy stencil.

When the paint has dried, paint on a light coat of varnish.

Leave the first coat to dry and apply another thin coat.

Ask an adult to clean the brush in turpentine as soon as you have finished.

This table mat has the corners cut off to make it a more interesting shape.

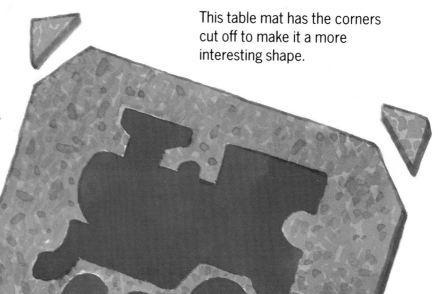

Stenciled Tin Cans

Use tin cans with removable lids. These are best for painting as they have no sharp edges. Clean the tin cans and make sure they are dry before you start to paint.

You will need:
enamel paints
paintbrush
turpentine

Paint the tin cans one color all over and leave to dry.

Hold the stencils against the sides of the tin cans with one hand and paint in the shapes with the other.

Stenciled tin cans can be used for desk organizers, gift boxes, cake and cookie tins or money boxes.

You can choose any of the stencils in this book to decorate tiles and tins.

STENCILS pp 68 · 74

Make Your Mark

Painting on fabric is really easy, and using stencils you can make matching T-shirts for your friends or family. Practice on an old T-shirt and remember that a little bit of paint goes a very long way.

You will need:
T-shirts
fabric paints
a flat-ended stencil brush
masking tape
a piece of cardboard
(to fit inside the T-shirt)
scissors

Cut the cardboard to the same size as the body of your T-shirt.

Put the cardboard inside the T-shirt to stretch it flat.

Tape the stencil down across the corners.

Paint through the stencil using an up-and-down dabbing movement. Follow the fabric paint maker's instructions. You may need to iron your design on so that it will not wash off.

Remove the stencil carefully and put the T-shirt on a hanger to dry.

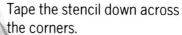

56

STENCILS pp 69·80

Trace around your hands to make this stencil.

Paint one hand and leave it to dry.

Clean the stencil, turn it over and paint the second hand.

A single star stencil looks good when used all over a T-shirt or vest.

Lighter Lamp Shades

An old lamp shade can be given a new look with stencils. The moon and stars would be nice on a bedroom lamp shade.

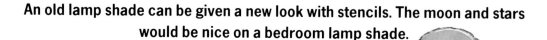

You will need:
a plain fabric or
  paper lamp shade
pencil
acrylic paints
paintbrush
masking tape

Before you paint, mark lightly with pencil where your moons and stars will go. This way they will not bump into each other as you move around the lamp shade.

Use masking tape to stick the stencil down before you paint. It will peel off easily.

Paint in the stencil and remove carefully.

Allow time for each stencil to dry before you start the next one. This way you will avoid smudges.

A designer lamp shade to smarten up any room

STENCILS p 80.

Fabulous Flowerpots

You can make a gift of a plant extra-special when you stencil the flowerpot.

You will need:	paintbrush
clay flowerpots	sponge
acrylic paints	masking tape

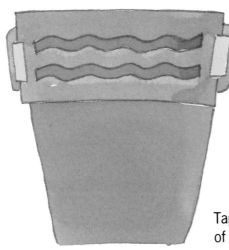

Tape the stencil to the top of the pot and paint it.

Leave it to dry and join another stencil to it, to give a pattern all the way around the top.

Stencil the spots all over the flowerpot, taking care not to smudge them.

Last of all, add a beautiful plant to make a really dazzling display.

STENCILS p 70

Puppet Theater

Put on a show for your friends with your own puppet theater made from just one cardboard box.

You will need
paints
paintbrush
masking tape
a few wooden spoons
thin poster board
a strong cardboard box
scissors

Cut off the flaps from the open end of the box and keep them.

Turn the box the other way up and cut out a rectangle at the front, near the top, for the stage.

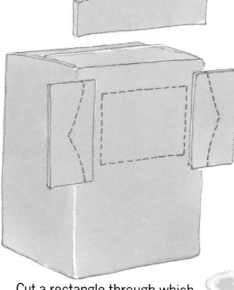

Cut a rectangle through which you will work the puppets. This is the back.

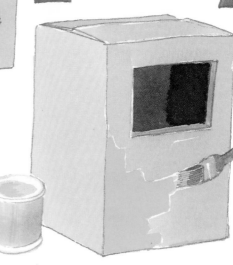

Cut the rooftop and the side curtains from the leftover flaps.

Paint the box one color and the curtains and roof another.

Decorate the roof with stenciled dots and a star. You could use glue and glitter on these as well.

STENCILS pp 70 · 74

Stencil on the stripes using the wavy line in a darker color.

Stencil a dot on each curtain and add the lines by hand to show the folds.

When all the paint is dry, glue the curtains and roof onto your theater.

Use the identikit stencils (see pages 36 & 37) to make your puppets.

Stencil onto thin poster board and cut them out.

Stick the wooden spoons onto the back of the poster board using masking tape.

Wacky Wall Border

Stencils are often used to paint a border around the top of a room. Using long strips of poster board, you can do the same and stick them, end to end, all around your room. This way you can change the pattern of your wall border as often as you like.

You will need:
- sheets of thin poster board
- pencil
- ruler
- scissors
- paints
- paintbrushes

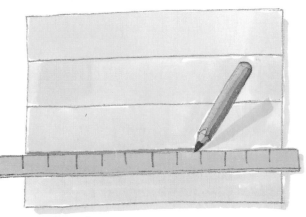

Take a sheet of poster board and divide two opposite edges into equal parts about 4″ (10 centimeters) each.

Draw lines across the sheet carefully, using a pencil and a ruler.

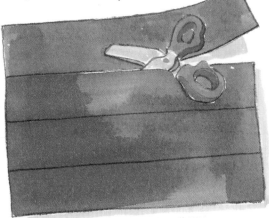

Cut along these lines with scissors. Now you have the strips of poster board to make your wall border.

Paint each strip separately, and when they are all dry, stick them to your wall, one next to the other, so that they make a continuous line around your room.

STENCILS pp 66 · 68 · 69 · 80

This stars-moons-and-planets wall border would look good in your bedroom, especially if you already have a stenciled moon-and-stars lamp shade.

Different flowers make a pretty border.

This train wall border can be made easily by starting with the locomotive and then stenciling the same pattern over and over again for the cars. Then you can draw people, children and animals looking out of the windows.

There's So Much More You Can Do . . .

In this book, we have shown you how to make stencils and how to decorate all sorts of surfaces and objects with them. But there are many more ideas that we didn't have room for. Here are a few extra, and there will be plenty of your own ideas that you will want to try out.

STENCILS pp 66 · 67 · 68 · 70 · 80

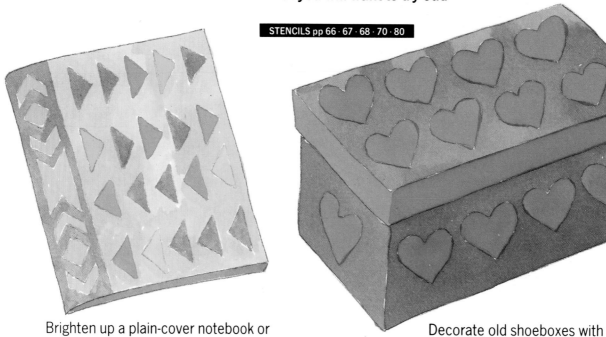

Brighten up a plain-cover notebook or drawing pad with stencils.

Decorate old shoeboxes with stencils to gift-wrap your Christmas or birthday presents.

A ribbon stenciled onto the corner of an old pillowcase will give it a new lease of life.

You can stencil bookmarks with all sorts of patterns to make a handmade present.

Now, have fun making up your own stencils!

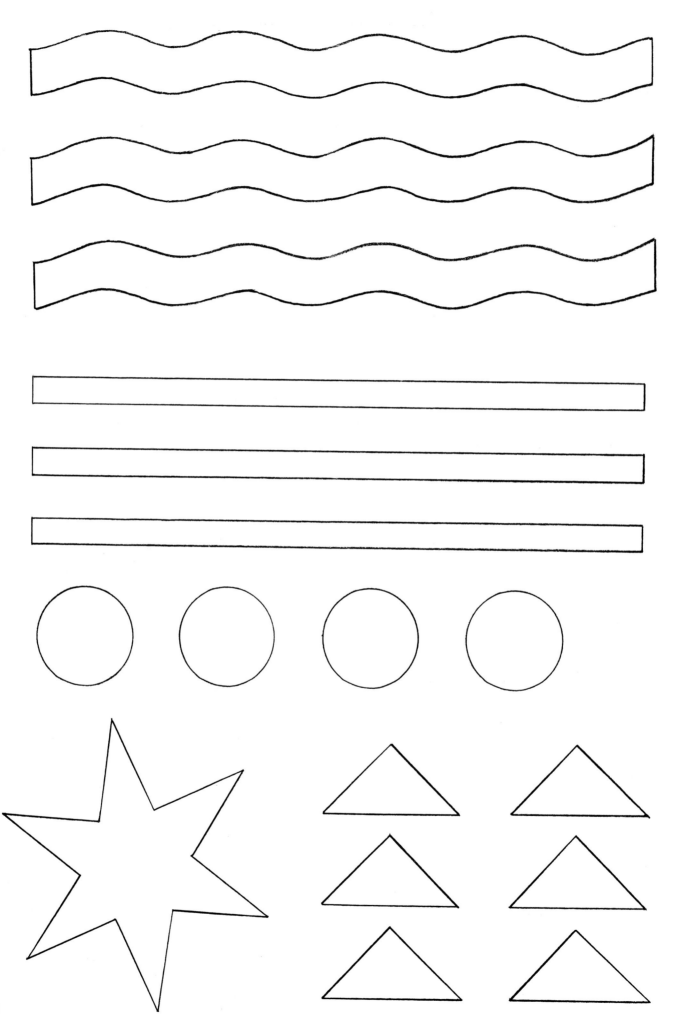

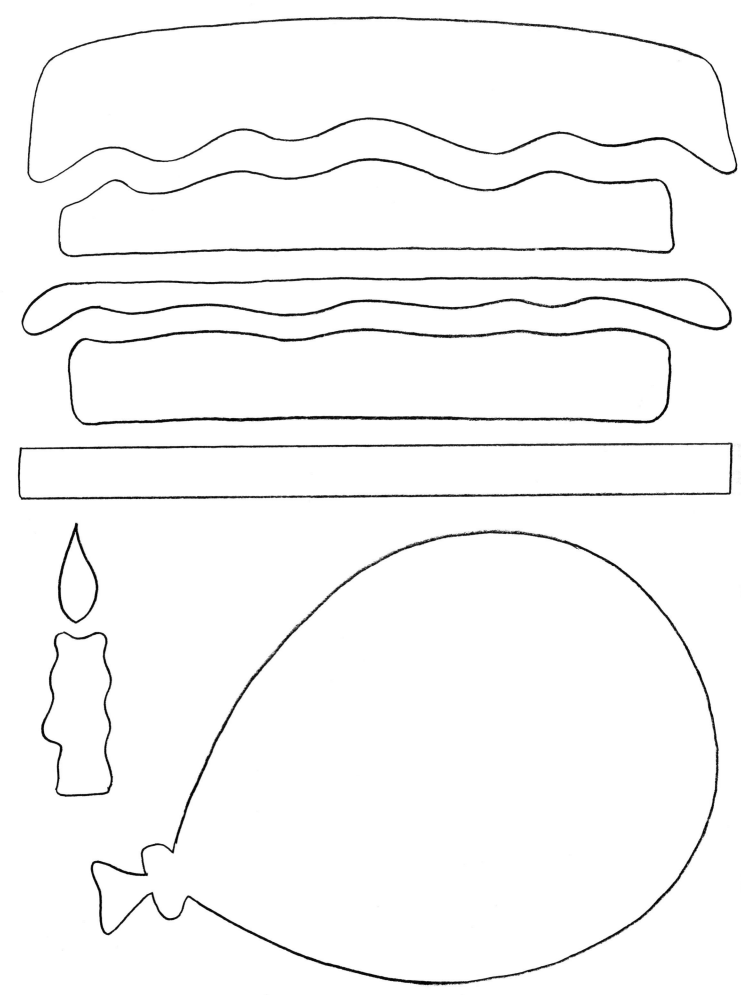